Essential ABCs
By

Breanna Griffin

First Edition: May 2023
Published in North America by Breanna Griffin.
Library of Congress Cataloguing-In-Publication Data 2013952224

Essential ABCs/Breanna Griffin – 1st ed

ISBN: 978-1-941859-90-2
1. JUVENILE NONFICTION / Concepts / Alphabet. 2. JUVENILE NONFICTION / Cooking & Food. 3. JUVENILE NONFICTION / Health & Daily Living / Diet & Nutrition. 4. JUVENILE NONFICTION / Reference / General. 5. JUVENILE NONFICTION / Science & Nature / Flowers & Plants.
10 9 8 7 6 5 4 3 2 1

Comments about Essential ABCs and requests for additional copies, book club rates and author speaking appearances may be addressed to Breanna Griffin or
you can send your comments and requests via e-mail to
Breannagriffin376@yahoo.com
Also available as an eBook from Internet retailers.
Printed in the United States of America

This book is dedicated to

Jaycee & *Justice*

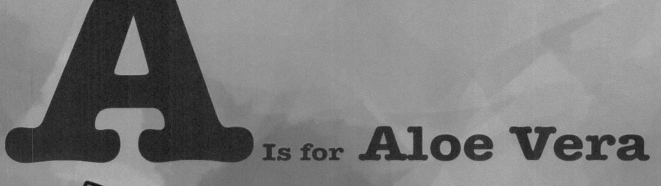

A Is for Aloe Vera

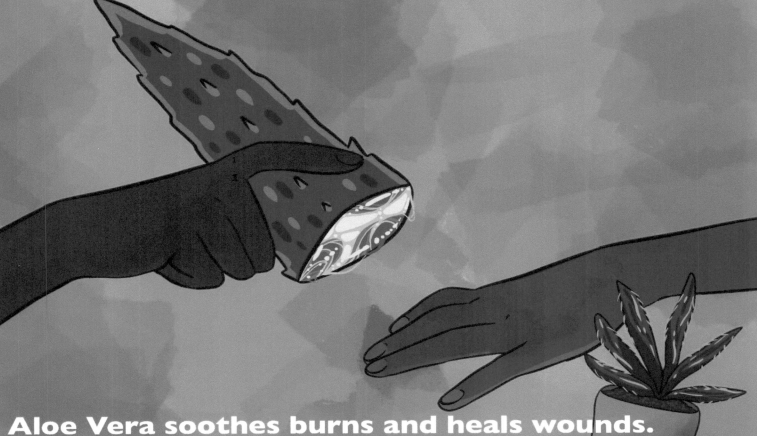

Aloe Vera soothes burns and heals wounds.
Whether it's sunburn, burns, cuts, and scrapes.

Bay Leaves are a good source of vitamin A, vitamin B6, and vitamin C.

B is for Bay Leaf

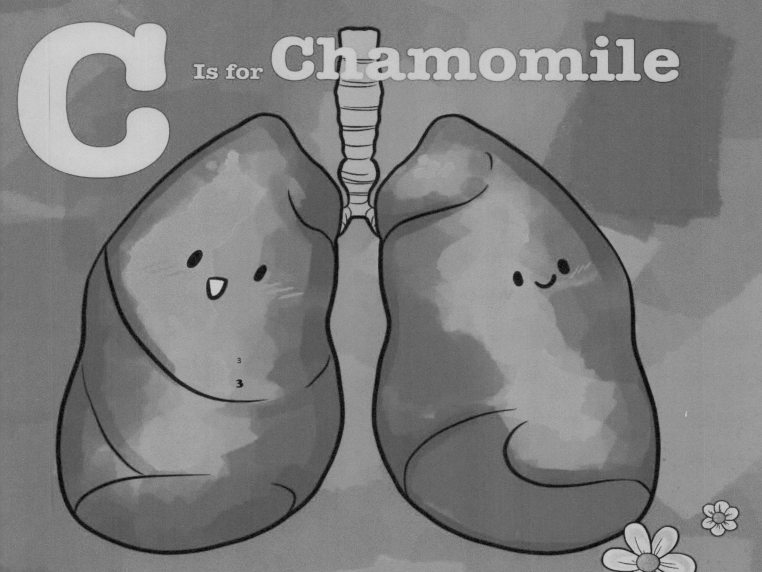

C IS for Chamomile

Chamomile treats inflammations of the skin and mucous membranes, for various bacterial infections of the skin, oral cavity and gums, and respiratory tract.

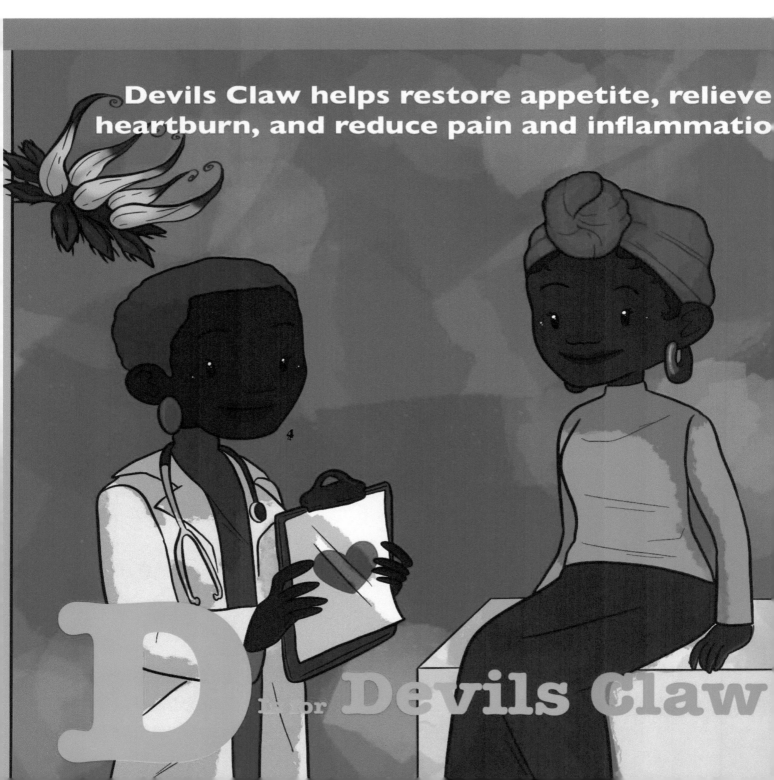

E Is for **Elder Flower**

Elder flower treats swollen sinuses, colds, common flu, swine flu, diabetes, and constipation.

Fever Few is promoted for fevers, headaches, and arthritis.

F **Is for** Fever Few

G Is for Ginger

Ginger root helps speed up the digestion process and empty your stomach more quickly.

Holy basil may help improve acne, reduce skin inflammation, and increase the speed of hair growth.

H Is for Holy Basil

I

Is for **Ice cream Bean fruit**

Ice cream beans are believed to help
stimulate digestion, relieve stomach
irritations, and act as an anti-inflammatory.

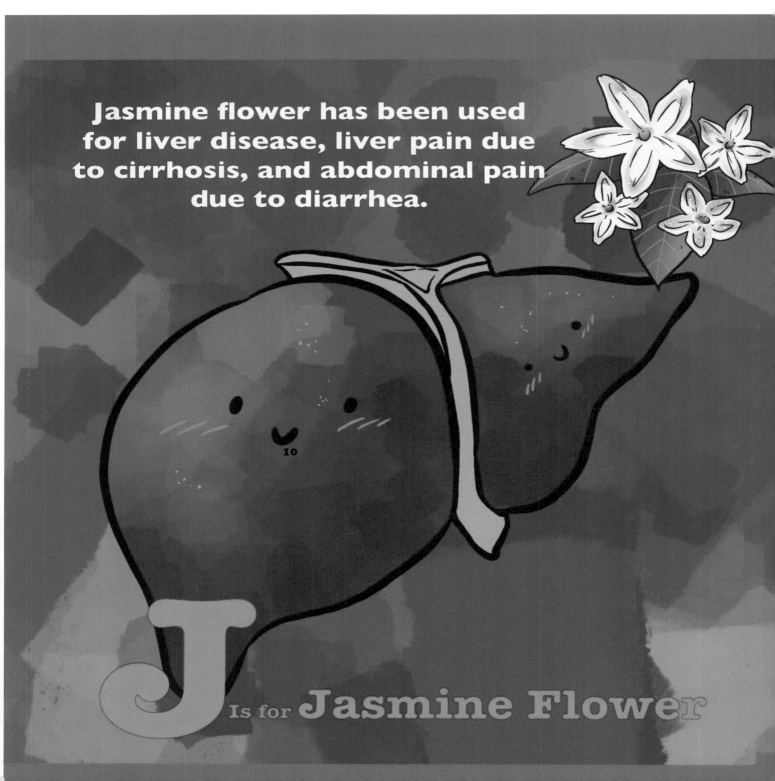

Jasmine flower has been used for liver disease, liver pain due to cirrhosis, and abdominal pain due to diarrhea.

J Is for Jasmine Flower

K Is for Kaffir Lime

Kaffir lime promotes oral health, detoxifies the blood, boost skin health, improve digestion, ward off insects, aid the immune system, reduce stress, and improve the health of hair.

Mint helps you with allergies and asthma. It is also a great remedy for the common cold, it boosts your immune system.

O Is for Oregano

Oregano also might help with digestion and with fighting against some bacteria and viruses.

Q Is for Quassia Mara

Quassia Mara is a plant. The wood is used as medicine. Quassia is used for treating an eating disorder called anorexia, indigestion, constipation, and fever.

Rosemary helps boost the immune system
and improve blood circulation.

R Is for Rosemary

S Is for Sea moss

19
19

Sea moss can assist your mental and emotional health, support your immune system, and aid in weight loss.

Turmeric is promoted as a dietary supplement for conditions including, arthritis, digestive disorders, respiratory infections, allergies, and liver disease.

T Is for **Turmeric**

U Is for Ugli Fruit

No more swollen feet!

Ugli fruit is low in calories and contains fiber and a variety of vitamins and minerals. It's also a very powerful anti-inflammatory antioxidants.

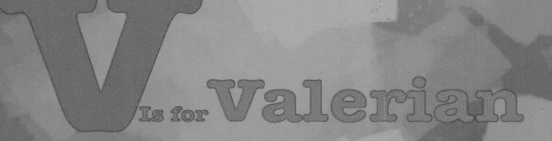

V **Is for Valerian**

Valerian root may help improve sleep quality, reduce anxiety, improve symptoms of OCD, and reduce hyperactive behavior in children.

White Willow bark is commonly used for back pain, fever, flu, muscle pain, and many other conditions.

23

W is for White Willow

Xigua, also known as watermelon, enhances blood flow and boosts circulation. Eat more watermelon!

X

Is for **Xigua**

Yerba buena can help get rid of bad breath. It helps relieve nasal congestion and it can help treat digestive problems.

Y Is for Yerba Buena

Zedoary is used for spasms, loss of appetite, and indigestion. Some people also use it for anxiety, stress, fatigue, pain, and swelling.

Z is for Zedoary

Now you know your essential !
ABC's

Printed in the USA
CPSIA information can be obtained
at www.ICGtesting.com
LVHW072149121023
760948LV00001B/1